THE
ULTIMATE GUIDE TO THE
PREMIER LEAGUE
2022

WRITTEN BY **ROB MASON**　　|　　DESIGNED BY **JODIE CLARK**

PBR

A Pillar Box Red Publication

© 2021. Published by Pillar Box Red Publishing Limited. Printed in the EU.

ISBN: 978-1-912456-91-8

Images © Alamy Live News.

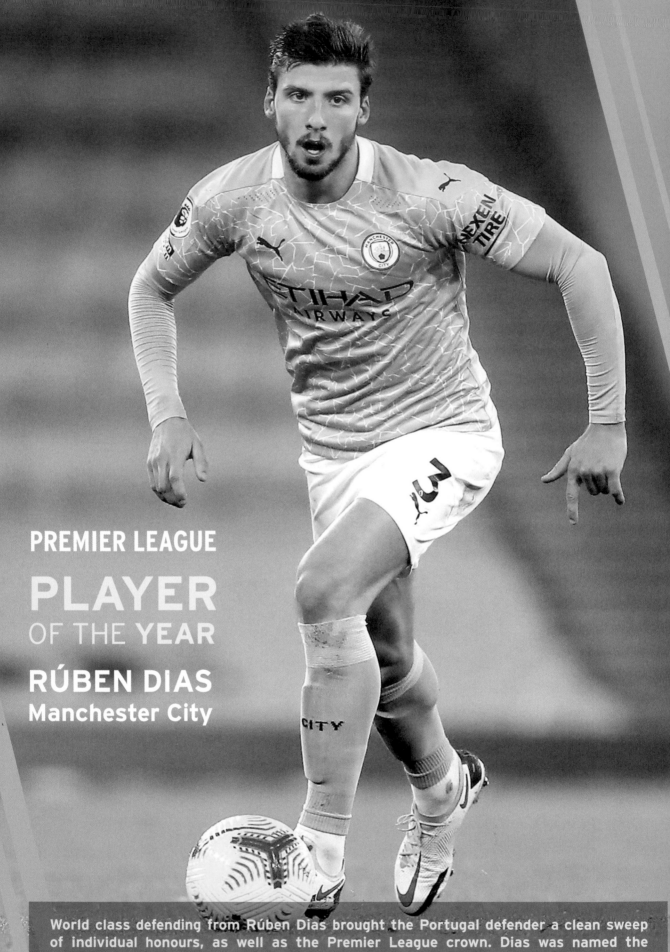

PREMIER LEAGUE

PLAYER
OF THE YEAR

RÚBEN DIAS
Manchester City

World class defending from Rúben Dias brought the Portugal defender a clean sweep of individual honours, as well as the Premier League crown. Dias was named the Premier League Player of the Year, the Football Writers' Association Player of the Year, Manchester City's Player of the Year and was named in the Premier League Team of the Season and, just for good measure, the UEFA Champions League Squad of the Season.

CONTENTS

This is the Premier League's best team according to the votes of the players themselves in the Professional Footballers' Association.

SHAW, Man Utd

United's Player of the Year and the creator of 72 Premier League chances, second only to Liverpool's Trent Alexander-Arnold.

DIAS, Man City

The Premier League Player of the Season. With him in the team, City let in 0.7 goals per game. Without him the figure was 1.8!

EDERSON, Man City

The Golden Glove winner for a second successive season and the first keeper to keep most clean sheets in two seasons since Joe Hart in 2013.

STONES, Man City

City conceded fewer goals with him on the pitch than any other defensive combination. With Stones barring the way, only one goal was scored per 161 minutes.

CANCELO, Man City

Effective defensively and the creator of more chances from open play than any defender.

FERNANDES, Man Utd

Not since Robin van Persie in 2012-13 has any United player equalled Fernandes' 30 goal involvements: 18 goals and 12 assists.

SON, Tottenham

His brilliant partnership with Kane brought 17 goals and 10 assists.

GÜNDOĞAN, Man City

Scored more non-penalty goals from midfield than anyone in the Premier League since Dele Alli in 2016-17, both notching 12 times.

KANE, Tottenham

23 goals. 14 assists. Seven more goal involvements than any other player. Fabulous.

DE BRUYNE, Man City

The only player to be named in this team for the last two seasons – and three times in total.

SALAH, Liverpool

Topped 20 Premier League goals in a season for the third time.

FANTASY XI

Many years ago, the best team was chosen from the English, Scottish, Irish and some foreign leagues for representative games to see who had the strongest league. This wouldn't happen now, as managers wouldn't be happy for their star players to add another big representative game to their crowded football calendars. But imagine...

GOALKEEPERS

Alisson
Ederson
Hugo Lloris
Emiliano Martínez
Edouard Mendy
Jordan Pickford
Nick Pope
Kasper Schmeichel

RIGHT BACKS

Trent Alexander-Arnold
Luke Ayling
Aaron Wan-Bissaka
Reece James
Tariq Lamptey
Kyle Walker

CENTRE BACKS

(Choose two)

Ruben Dias
Virgil van Dijk
Wesley Fofana
Aymeric Laporte
Harry Maguire
Antonio Rüdiger
Caglar Soyuncu
John Stones

LEFT BACKS

Ben Chilwell
Lucas Digne
Sergio Reguilón
Andy Robertson
Luke Shaw
Kieran Tierney

LEFT BACK

CENTRE BACK

CENTRE BACK

GOAL KEEPER

RIGHT BACK

Imagine you could pick a Premier League team to play a best team from Spain, Germany, France or Italy.
Who would you choose?

Fill in your team sheet here by choosing anyone you like from the Premier League. You don't have to choose from the shortlists here; these are just suggestions!

Would your team beat the best of LaLiga, the Bundesliga, Ligue 1 or Serie A? You bet it would – this is the Premier League.

MIDFIELDER

FORWARD

MIDFIELDER

FORWARD

MIDFIELDER

FORWARD

MANAGER

FORWARDS
(Choose three)
Pierre-Emerick Aubameyang
Patrick Bamford
Dominic Calvert-Lewin
Roberto Firmino
Phil Foden
Mason Greenwood
Son Heung-min
Danny Ings
Harry Kane
Riyad Mahrez
Sadio Mane
Marcus Rashford
Mo Salah
Raheem Sterling
Jamie Vardy
Wilfried Zaha

MIDFIELDERS
(Choose three)
Kevin De Bruyne
Bruno Fernandes
Jack Grealish
İlkay Gündoğan
Jordan Henderson
Pierre-Emile Hojbjerg
N'Golo Kanté
James Maddison
Mason Mount
Wilfred Ndidi
Kalvin Phillips
Paul Pogba
Youri Tielemans

AND WHO WOULD YOUR MANAGER BE?
Pep Guardiola
Jürgen Klopp
Brendan Rodgers
Ole Gunnar Solskjaer
Thomas Tuchel

9

GOLDEN BOOT

Perhaps the best striker in the world, Harry Kane didn't just top the Premier League scorers list in 2020/21 with 23 goals, he was also the Premier League's top playmaker with 14 assists! His partnership with Son Heung-min saw Son become the league's fourth top scorer with 17 Premier League goals. The pair provided 40 of Spurs' total of 68 Premier League goals. In 38 games, Tottenham only scored 31 goals that did not involve Hero Harry.

Being the most feared man in the Premier League, Kane is tightly marked but still manages to score all manner of goals: right-foot, left-foot, headers, close-range, long-range, set-pieces and open play. Harry Kane is the perfect all-round centre-forward.

TOTAL PREMIER LEAGUE GOALS:	23
PREMIER LEAGUE HOME GOALS:	12
PREMIER LEAGUE AWAY GOALS:	11
NUMBER OF PREMIER LEAGUE CLUBS SCORED AGAINST:	16
NUMBER OF PREMIER LEAGUE GAMES SCORED IN:	18
GOALS SCORED AGAINST TOP FOUR:	2
GOALS SCORED AGAINST BOTTOM THREE:	4

TEEAMS SCORED AGAINST

ARSENAL	1
ASTON VILLA	1
BRIGHTON	1
BURNLEY	1
CRYSTAL PALACE	3
EVERTON	2
FULHAM	1
LEEDS UNITED	1
LEICESTER CITY	1
MANCHESTER UNITED	2
NEWCASTLE UNITED	2
SHEFFIELD UNITED	1
SOUTHAMPTON	1
WEST BROMWICH ALBION	2
WEST HAM UNITED	2
WOLVERHAMPTON WANDERERS	1

JUST FOR GOOD MEASURE

EUROPA LEAGUE GOALS	8
CARABAO CUP GOALS	1
FA CUP GOALS	1
INTERNATIONAL GOALS	2*
TOTAL GOALS FOR 2020/21	35*

*Does not include any goals scored in the Summer European Championships.

CRYSTAL PALACE & WBA:
Teams scored against home and away

CLIMBING HIGHER

At the start of the 2020/21 season, Kane was the seventh highest ever scorer in the Premier League with 166 goals. If he matches his 2020/21 tally of 23 goals, he will climb above Thierry Henry, Frank Lampard, Sergio Agüero and Andy Cole to become the third top scorer in Premier League history. Having turned 28 just before the start of the season, Harry is young enough to go on and overtake the Premier League's highest ever scorers Wayne Rooney (208) and Alan Shearer (260).

GOLDEN GLOVE

EDERSON, MANCHESTER CITY

There was a time when Brazil was considered to be by far the best team in the world, but their goalkeepers were considered their one weak link. Not anymore! For the last three years the Premier League Golden Glove has been awarded to goalkeepers from Brazil. In 2021, Manchester City's Ederson retained the title that he took from his countryman Alisson, who won it with Liverpool in 2019.

Playing behind the Champions' defence means that Ederson doesn't have so many shots to save as, say, a goalkeeper playing for a struggling side, but he has to keep his concentration for when he is needed. As any goalkeeper will tell you, that can be harder than being involved all the time when your team is under pressure. Not only is Ederson a wonderfully agile and brave goalkeeper, but he is also superb when he has the ball. As well as being City's last line of defence, Ederson is also their first line of attack. Usually he will play a short ball to one of his defenders as Pep Guardiola's side like to build from the back, but if opponents squeeze up on City with a high press, Ederson's ability to hit a piercingly accurate long pass can set his forwards clean through on the opposition goal.

Last season, Ederson kept 19 clean sheets; three more than he had achieved the previous year. In 2019/20, Alisson went unbeaten 21 times, which means the two Brazilians have kept more clean sheets in a season than anyone in the last 3 years since 2008/09, when Manchester United's Edwin van der Sar kept 21. The only season this has been bettered was in the very first year of the Golden Glove award when Chelsea's Petr Čech kept an incredible 24 Premier League shut-outs.

TOTAL PREMIER LEAGUE CLEAN SHEETS:	19
PREMIER LEAGUE HOME CLEAN SHEETS:	10
PREMIER LEAGUE AWAY CLEAN SHEETS	9
NUMBER OF PREMIER LEAGUE CLUBS CLEAN SHEETS KEPT AGAINST:	14
CLEAN SHEETS AGAINST THE REST OF THE TOP FOUR:	1
GOALS SCORED AGAINST BOTTOM THREE:	5

TEAMS CLEAN SHEETS KEPT AGAINST

ARSENAL	2
ASTON VILLA	1
BRIGHTON	1
BURNLEY	2
CRYSTAL PALACE	2
EVERTON	1
FULHAM	2
LEICESTER CITY	1
MANCHESTER UNITED	1
NEWCASTLE UNITED	1
SHEFFIELD UNITED	2
SOUTHAMPTON	1
TOTTENHAM HOTSPUR	1
WEST BROMWICH ALBION	1

JUST FOR GOOD MEASURE

CHAMPIONS LEAGUE CLEAN SHEETS	7
CARABAO CUP CLEAN SHEETS	0*
FA CUP CLEAN SHEETS	0*
INTERNATIONAL CLEAN SHEETS	0*
TOTAL CLEAN SHEETS FOR 2020/21	26

*No appearances

CLIMBING HIGHER

If Ederson (or Alisson) wins the Golden Glove in 2021/22 then Brazil will draw level with England, Spain and the Czech Republic in having had players who have won the Golden Glove four times. Joe Hart is the only British goalkeeper to win the Golden Glove award. He won it four times with Manchester City. The Czech Republic's Petr Čech has also won four Golden Gloves, the first three with Chelsea and the last, in 2015/16, with Arsenal.

If Ederson becomes the Golden Glove holder for a third successive season, he will equal Pepe Reina of Liverpool and Spain as the only man to do so for three seasons in a row. Reina did so from 2006 to 2008.

Only five clubs have ever had a Golden Glove winner: Manchester City (6), Chelsea (4), Liverpool (4), Arsenal (2) and Manchester United (2).

PLAYERS OF THE MONTH

Bruno Fernandes and İlkay Gündoğan both won the Premier League Player of the Month award in back-to back months, while the last two awards of the season were awarded to players who were on loan!

SEPTEMBER 2020
DOMINIC CALVERT-LEWIN / EVERTON

PREMIER LEAGUE GAMES	3
PREMIER LEAGUE GOALS	5
PREMIER LEAGUE ASSISTS	0
PREMIER LEAGUE POINTS WON	9

Calvert-Lewin kicked off the season in a hurry. He scored in all three of his Premier League games, including a hat-trick against West Bromwich Albion. The on-fire front man also scored a League Cup hat-trick against West Ham United on the last day of the month.

OCTOBER 2020
SON HEUNG-MIN / TOTTENHAM HOTSPUR

PREMIER LEAGUE GAMES	3
PREMIER LEAGUE GOALS	4
PREMIER LEAGUE ASSISTS	2
PREMIER LEAGUE POINTS WON	7

The superb South Korean started October with two goals in Spurs' stunning 6-1 win at Manchester United. He followed this up with goals in his next two games, in a draw with West Ham and a headed winner at Burnley. Adding two assists to his four-goal haul, Son was a worthy winner.

NOVEMBER 2020
BRUNO FERNANDES / MANCHESTER UNITED

PREMIER LEAGUE GAMES	4
PREMIER LEAGUE GOALS	4
PREMIER LEAGUE ASSISTS	1
PREMIER LEAGUE POINTS WON	9

The Portugal playmaker produced two goals in United's win at Everton and also scored in victories over West Brom and Southampton. Just for good measure, he also weighed in with a couple of Champions League goals.

DECEMBER 2020
BRUNO FERNANDES / MANCHESTER UNITED

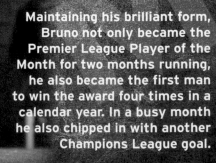

PREMIER LEAGUE GAMES	5
PREMIER LEAGUE GOALS	3
PREMIER LEAGUE ASSISTS	4
PREMIER LEAGUE POINTS WON	11

Maintaining his brilliant form, Bruno not only became the Premier League Player of the Month for two months running, he also became the first man to win the award four times in a calendar year. In a busy month he also chipped in with another Champions League goal.

JANUARY 2021
İLKAY GÜNDOĞAN / MANCHESTER CITY

PREMIER LEAGUE GAMES	6
PREMIER LEAGUE GOALS	5
PREMIER LEAGUE ASSISTS	0
PREMIER LEAGUE POINTS WON	18

Gündoğan got City's first goal of 2021 in a 3-1 win at Chelsea and just kept going. He also scored in big wins over Palace and West Brom, where he got two. There was also a last-minute penalty in a comfortable win over Aston Villa, not to mention more good performances in domestic cup victories over Manchester United and Cheltenham.

FEBRUARY 2021
İLKAY GÜNDOĞAN / MANCHESTER CITY

PREMIER LEAGUE GAMES	5
PREMIER LEAGUE GOALS	4
PREMIER LEAGUE ASSISTS	1
PREMIER LEAGUE POINTS WON	15

Having seen United's Bruno Fernandes win the Premier League Player of the Month award in November and December, Gündoğan became the first Manchester City player to win the award in successive months. He scored twice against reigning champions Liverpool 4-1 at Anfield and a week later netted twice as Spurs were humbled in Manchester.

MARCH 2021
KELECHI IHEANACHO / LEICESTER CITY

PREMIER LEAGUE GAMES	3
PREMIER LEAGUE GOALS	5
PREMIER LEAGUE ASSISTS	0
PREMIER LEAGUE POINTS WON	7

Beginning March with a goal in a 1-1 draw at Burnley, Iheanacho hit a rich vein of form. Three days later he scored in a narrow win at Brighton and then followed up with a hat-trick as a doomed Sheffield United was beaten 5-0. Add two more goals to all this in an FA Cup win over Manchester United during the Foxes run to winning the trophy.

APRIL 2021
JESSE LINGARD / WEST HAM UNITED

PREMIER LEAGUE GAMES	3
PREMIER LEAGUE GOALS	4
PREMIER LEAGUE ASSISTS	1
PREMIER LEAGUE POINTS WON	6

On loan from Manchester United, Jesse Lingard was in outstanding form for West Ham. Beginning the month with a goal at Molineux (where Wolves were beaten), Lingard followed up with a brace as Leicester City were beaten and also scored in a defeat at Newcastle.

MAY 2021
JOE WILLOCK / NEWCASTLE UNITED

PREMIER LEAGUE GAMES	4
PREMIER LEAGUE GOALS	4
PREMIER LEAGUE ASSISTS	0
PREMIER LEAGUE POINTS WON	9

On loan from Arsenal, Joe Willock scored in all four of his games in May. Incredibly this took his record to a goal a game in all of his last seven games of the season - a feat that equalled Alan Shearer's record for the Magpies.

MANAGERS OF THE MONTH

The first three managers of the month were no longer with their clubs by the following summer, but all of these bosses enjoyed success during 2020/21.

SEPTEMBER 2020
CARLO ANCELOTTI / EVERTON

The new Everton manager made a 100% start to the season and added this award to the four he had won previously with Chelsea. Impressive wins in the capital at Tottenham and Crystal Palace came either side of a five goal Goodison display against newly promoted West Bromwich Albion. The Toffees' 100% September start was matched by three victories in the League Cup, including a 4-1 thrashing of West Ham United.

| PREMIER LEAGUE GAMES | 3 |
| PREMIER LEAGUE POINTS WON | 9 |

OCTOBER 2020
NUNO ESPÍRITO SANTO / WOLVERHAMPTON WANDERERS

After a disappointing September, Wolves looked like they had returned to the form they showed the previous season as the 10th month of the year saw them pick up 10 points. Only one goal was conceded by former goalkeeper Nuno Espírito Santo's side as they were held to a draw by Newcastle. Clean sheets were the building block of 1-0 wins over newly promoted Fulham and Leeds, as well as a 2-0 crushing of Crystal Palace.

| PREMIER LEAGUE GAMES | 4 |
| PREMIER LEAGUE POINTS WON | 10 |

NOVEMBER 2020
JOSÉ MOURINHO / TOTTENHAM HOTSPUR

José Mourinho showed his 'Special One' credentials with a spectacular month that included a 2-0 win over Manchester City and a tactically astute goalless draw at his old club, Chelsea. Three-point hauls against Brighton and West Brom meant Spurs ended November top of the Premier League table, having also progressed in the Europa League by winning both of their games.

| PREMIER LEAGUE GAMES | 4 |
| PREMIER LEAGUE POINTS WON | 10 |

DECEMBER 2020
DEAN SMITH / ASTON VILLA

Life-long Villa supporter Dean Smith claimed his first Premier League Manager of the Month award. Only in the last game of the month at Chelsea did Villa concede, although an excellent point was still gleaned from a 1-1 draw. Earlier in December there had been a 1-0 win at Wolves, a goalless draw against Burnley and back-to-back 3-0 wins over West Brom and Crystal Place either side of a happy Christmas.

| PREMIER LEAGUE GAMES | 5 |
| PREMIER LEAGUE POINTS WON | 11 |

JANUARY 2021
PEP GUARDIOLA /
MANCHESTER CITY

PREMIER LEAGUE GAMES	6
PREMIER LEAGUE POINTS WON	18

Pep Guardiola's eventual Premier League champions went into overdrive as the new calendars were put up. Having ended 2020 with back to back Premier League wins, they kept a 100% record in six Premier League games against Chelsea, Brighton, Palace, Villa, WBA and Sheffield United, sticking four past Palace and five past West Brom. With three cup wins in the month as well, including one at local rivals United, the City slickers slipped into top gear.

FEBRUARY 2021
PEP GUARDIOLA /
MANCHESTER CITY

PREMIER LEAGUE GAMES	5
PREMIER LEAGUE POINTS WON	15

Burnley, Liverpool, Spurs, Everton and Arsenal were all swept aside as the City machine established a 10-point gap at the top of the Premier League by the end of the month. Only one of those games was at home, with a 4-1 demolition of reigning champions Liverpool at Anfield signalling that it would be City who would capture the Premier League crown. For Guardiola, it was the ninth time he had been named Manager of the Month.

MARCH 2021
THOMAS TUCHEL /
CHELSEA

PREMIER LEAGUE GAMES	3
PREMIER LEAGUE POINTS WON	7

Having taken over at Stamford Bridge in late January, Thomas Tuchel took his first Manager of the Month award after beating Merseyside rivals Liverpool at Anfield and Everton in London without conceding a goal. Following that up with a goalless draw at Leeds, Chelsea's Premier League involvement was over before the month was half way through. They kept their defensive tightness by not conceding as they went on to win games in both the Champions League and FA Cup en-route to both finals.

APRIL 2021
STEVE BRUCE /
NEWCASTLE UNITED

PREMIER LEAGUE GAMES	4
PREMIER LEAGUE POINTS WON	8

A long-awaited first Premier League Manager of the Month award was richly deserved by Steve Bruce, who continued his hard-fought challenge of winning over many fans of the team he supported in boyhood. Always more tactically astute than many give him credit for, Steve masterminded solid wins at Burnley and at home to West Ham and finished the month unbeaten, having engineered points from difficult fixtures against Tottenham and Liverpool.

MAY 2021
JÜRGEN KLOPP /
LIVERPOOL

PREMIER LEAGUE GAMES	5
PREMIER LEAGUE POINTS WON	15

Having failed to consistently replicate the scintillating form that made them champions in 2020, Liverpool ended the season by reminding everyone of how good they can be and shot up to a final position of third in the table. Beginning and ending the month with 2-0 home wins over Southampton and Crystal Palace, in between they won at old rivals Manchester United as well as West Brom and Burnley.

SPOT THE

Can you work out which Premier League season this is?

FIND THE ANSWER ON PAGE 61.

With seconds left of the season, and United hoping they were champions after the final whistle had gone on their last day win at Sunderland, rivals City came from behind to beat QPR even though they had been behind in the 90th minute!

This season was officially named the "Best Season in the First 20 Years of the Premier League".

The title winning goal in the dying seconds of the season was scored by Sergio Agüero with the commentator screaming,

"AGÜEROOOOOOOO!"

as the ball sensationally hit the net.

Newcastle also won the Goal of the Season award through Papiss Cissé for his second goal in a 2-0 win at Chelsea.

It was City's first Premier League title, making them the fifth club to be Premier League champions.

City had won 6-1 away to United.

Manchester enjoyed dominance in North London, United winning 8-2 at Arsenal and City triumphing 5-1 at Spurs.

Arsenal joined both Manchester clubs in qualifying for the Champions League along with Chelsea who won the Champions League in this season.

SEASON

During this season Marc Albrighton of Aston Villa scored the 20,000th goal in the history of the Premier League.

Play-off winners Swansea City became the first non-English club to play in the Premier League. They had the best disciplinary record in their first season with only 39 yellow cards and just two reds as they won the Fair Play award.

Arsenal's Robin van Persie was the Premier League's top scorer with 30 goals.

The title was decided on goal difference after the top two teams Manchester City and Manchester United were level on 89 points.

Manchester City's Joe Hart won the Golden Glove award for 17 clean sheets.

Vincent Kompany of Manchester City was the Premier League Player of the Year.

Blackburn Rovers, Bolton Wanderers and Wolves were relegated.

Newcastle United's Alan Pardew was Manager of the Year.

NORWICH CITY'S supporters were named the BEST BEHAVED in the Premier League.

ANSWER

ARE YOU

NORWICH CITY

The Championship champion Canaries will hope to do better this time round after suffering relegation in 2020/21, having won the Championship the previous season.

REASONS WHY THEY WILL GO DOWN

TEEMU PUKKI: Pukki scored 29 goals as City won the Championship in 2019 but, once in with the big boys of the Premier League, scored only 11 times. Only two of those came after Christmas when teams had worked him out, and defences already know how to deal with him this time round.

DANIEL FARKE: Norwich showed loyalty in not sacking Farke when they went straight back down after coming into the Premier League two seasons ago, but this time should they ruthlessly go for a new face with fresh ideas and more experience in coping with the top level?

EXPERIENCE: Norwich couldn't cope in 2019/20 when they set a record fifth relegation from the Premier League. Trying again with largely the same squad, same head coach and same philosophy risks seeing the Canaries extending their own record of relegations.

YOUNG TALENT: Coping with the pace and power of the Premier League is something that often sees top overseas stars need time to get used to the top-level game in England, so thrusting too many promising youngsters into the fray is asking for trouble.

LACK OF GOALS: Last time at the top, Teemu Pukki and Todd Cantwell scored 11 and 6 Premier League goals, but no one else managed more than one. They have to get more goals from around the team, and that is easier said than done.

REASONS WHY THEY WILL STAY UP

TEEMU PUKKI: The Finnish finisher gives the Canaries class up front. He scored 26 goals as the Championship was won and every team needs a goal-scorer.

DANIEL FARKE: The German head coach has guided the Canaries to the Championship title in two of the last three seasons and has got the best out of his squad.

EXPERIENCE: Having had a season in the Premier League between their two Championship successes, this time around the Canaries are better equipped to know what is in store. They will have learned more about how to get results instead of simply playing nice football and (sometimes) being a soft touch to score against.

YOUNG TALENT: The Canaries have fledgling footballers such as Bali Mumba, Adam Idah, Andrew Omobamidele and Josh Martin, any of whom could be big names by the end of 2021/22.

YOUR PREDICTION OF NORWICH'S FINAL POSITION:

READY?

WATFORD

The Hornets won automatic promotion at the first time of asking. Their previous Premier League spell lasted for five seasons and they are capable of re-establishing themselves.

REASONS WHY THEY WILL STAY UP

CHANGING THE MANAGER / HEAD COACH: Unlike Norwich who have stuck with Daniel Farke through promotions and relegations, in recent seasons Watford have always been quick to fire failing bosses and bring in new ideas to spark their side.

MASSIVE PLAYER TURNOVER: Watford constantly re-invent themselves and never stand still. These days almost all clubs change players more regularly than they used to, but Watford are exceptional. This means players always have to strive to give their best or they know they'll be out.

NEW SIGNINGS: Sporting director Cristiano Giaretta is well experienced on the continent, especially in Italy and Bulgaria, and will be able to bring in players of the quality needed.

DEFENCE: Watford had the best defence in the Championship last season. They conceded just 30 goals in 46 games, with the fewest let in both at home and away. It was a most miserly record they will hope to build on in the Premier League.

HOME RECORD: Watford won 19 out of 23 home games in the promotion season, drawing two of the other four. No one scored as many goals at home (44) or conceded as few (just 12).

REASONS WHY THEY WILL GO DOWN

CHANGING THE MANAGER / HEAD COACH: Xisco Muñoz is the 13th gaffer Watford has had since parting company with Sean Dyche in 2012. Too much change means a lack of consistency.

MASSIVE PLAYER TURNOVER: Last season Watford brought in 19 new faces (including two on loan). They also bade farewell to 29 players, as well as dealing with an amazing 23 outward loans. Developing understanding on the pitch and team spirit is difficult if the team changes too much.

NEW SIGNINGS: Chances are that many of Watford's newcomers may be new to English football and it can take time to get used to playing in the Premier League – time Watford won't have if they are to stay up.

LACK OF A GREAT GOAL-SCORER: Promotion with a top scorer with only 13 goals in Ismaïla Sarr doesn't bode well for a team needing goals in the Premier League.

AWAY GOALS: Even relegated Wycombe scored more than Watford, who managed under a goal a game away from Vicarage Road as they won promotion. If they found goals on the road difficult in the Championship, the Premier League may be a step too far.

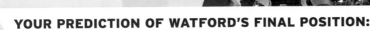

YOUR PREDICTION OF WATFORD'S FINAL POSITION:

ARE YOU READY?

BRENTFORD

Play-off victors Brentford became the 50th club to join the Premier League when they secured promotion to play for the first time and the top-flight for the first time since 1946-47.

REASONS WHY THEY WILL STAY UP

IVAN TONEY: They have a natural goal-scorer in Ivan Toney. He scored 33 times in total last term.

GOALS: They have goals throughout the team, with 17 different players getting a goal last season in all competitions.

HISTORY: Over half the teams ever promoted to the Premier League through the play-offs have stayed up in their first season.

CALMNESS: The Bees are a busy side who play good, composed football and have faith in their style of play.

LUCK: They were unlucky not to be promoted in 2019/20 and have looked like a Premier League team in-waiting for a year.

HEAD COACH: Head coach Thomas Frank will bring fresh ideas to the Premier League.

SURPRISE FACTOR: Being a team on a new adventure will give the Bees a surprise factor.

BRAND NEW STADIUM: Not only will Brentford have their fans back to relish top-class football, but they will enjoy the first full season at their brand-new Brentford Community Stadium.

REASONS WHY THEY WILL GO DOWN

INEXPERIENCE: Inexperienced at Premier League level, Brentford may struggle to cope with the relentless demands of a Premier League campaign.

TOO MANY DERBIES: Ten of their 38 games will be London derbies, and having over a quarter of their fixtures with that added intensity will add to the strains of coping with a higher level of football than they have been used to.

SQUAD SIZE: Brentford's first XI have decent quality but as injuries, suspensions and fatigue mount, will they be able to maintain that quality if they are without several regular players?

IVAN TONEY: If they lose Toney they may lack a regular scorer. Last season, no one other than Toney managed double-figures in terms of goals in the Championship.

LOSS OF PLAYERS: They have lost Emiliano Marcondes, who scored the play-off final goal that took the Bees into the Premier League. Although he was often a substitute, Marcondes often had a key impact on games.

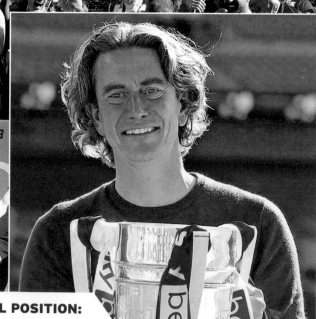

YOUR PREDICTION OF BRENTFORD'S FINAL POSITION:

PREMIER PREDICTIONS

Where do you think each team will finish in the Premier League this season?

Fill in the chart with your predictions. At the end of the season, compare the final table with how you thought the league would finish and see how many you got right.

	MY PREDICTION	ACTUAL RESULT
1st		
2nd		
3rd		
4th		
5th		
6th		
7th		
8th		
9th		
10th		
11th		
12th		
13th		
14th		
15th		
16th		
17th		
18th		
19th		
20th		

ARSENAL
ASTON VILLA
BRENTFORD
BRIGHTON & HOVE ALBION
BURNLEY
CHELSEA
CRYSTAL PALACE

EVERTON
LEEDS UNITED
LEICESTER CITY
LIVERPOOL
MANCHESTER CITY
MANCHESTER UNITED
NEWCASTLE UNITED

NORWICH CITY
SOUTHAMPTON
TOTTENHAM HOTSPUR
WATFORD
WEST HAM UNITED
WOLVERHAMPTON
WANDERERS

MEET THE CHAMPIONS

MANCHESTER CITY

POSITION:
CHAMPIONS

TOP SCORER:
İlkay Gündoğan (13)

PLAYER OF THE YEAR:
Rúben Dias

BIGGEST WINS:

MANCHESTER CITY **5-0** BURNLEY
WEST BROMWICH ALBION **0-5** MANCHESTER CITY
MANCHESTER CITY **5-0** EVERTON

BIGGEST DEFEAT:

MANCHESTER CITY **2-5** LEICESTER CITY

QUIZ QUESTION:

Other than top scorer Gündoğan, who was the only City player to reach double figures in Premier League goals?

ANSWER

(Answer on page 61)

WHAT THEY DID BETTER THAN ANYONE

- The best ever Premier League start to a calendar year: 13 consecutive victories from the beginning of January.
- Scored more goals at home than anyone else.
- Scored more goals away than anyone else.
- Conceded fewer goals at home than anyone else.
- Conceded fewer goals away than anyone else.
- Had a goal difference 22 better than the second-best side.
- Finished 12 points clear of their nearest rivals.
- Formed over half the PFA Premier League Team of the Year.
- Equalled the Premier League record of 11 successive away wins. Chelsea in 2008 and City themselves in 2017 are the only teams to achieve this.
- Their Under 23 and Under 18 teams won their Premier League titles too!

TAKING THE TITLE

CHELSEA 1-3 MANCHESTER CITY
Sunday 3 January 2021

Despite missing several men due to coronavirus, City demolished their future Champions League final opponents with three goals in a sensational 16-minute first half spell. Chelsea's late goal was barely a consolation as City climbed to fifth in the table.

GOALCHART

GÜNDOĞAN	0-1	18m
FODEN	0-2	21m
DE BRUYNE	0-3	34m
Hudson-Odoi	1-3	90+2m

LIVERPOOL 1-4 MANCHESTER CITY
Sunday 7 February 2021

A decisive win against the defending champions as City won at Anfield for the first time since 2003 and equalled Preston in 1892 and Arsenal in 1987 by registering a 14th successive victory. Ilkay Gündoğan had missed a first half penalty but opened the scoring and restored the lead after Liverpool levelled. Phil Foden was at his imperious best with his strike getting goal of the game, taking which took City five points clear at the pinnacle of the Premier – and with a game in hand.

GOALCHART

GÜNDOĞAN	0-1	49m
Salah	1-1	63m (P)
GÜNDOĞAN	1-2	73m
STERLING	1-3	76m
FODEN	1-4	83m

MANCHESTER CITY 3-0 SPURS
Saturday 13 February 2021

José Mourinho's Spurs were top when they defeated City earlier in the season, but were well beaten by slick City who took their tally to 41 points out of a possible 45 since the previous meeting. Ederson didn't have much to do in goal but managed to be a threat to Spurs. After Pep Guardiola had recently suggested the keeper might take a penalty, Ederson came forward, looking to take the spot-kick from which Rodri opened the scoring, and then claimed an assist for a brilliant long pass for Gündoğan to double the lead, before the German wrapped up the game with his ninth goal in his last nine Premier League games.

GOALCHART

RODRI	1-0	23m (P)	
GÜNDOĞAN	2-0	50m	
GÜNDOĞAN	3-0	66m	

EVERTON 1-3 MANCHESTER CITY
Wednesday 17 February 2021

City set yet another record, becoming the first top-flight team to ever win their first 10 games in a calendar year, as they stretched the lead at the top of the table to 10 points. Conceding an equaliser soon after taking the lead propelled City into extra gear, which saw them cruise past Carlo Ancelotti's impressive side, though England keeper Jordan Pickford kept the score down.

GOALCHART

FODEN	0-1	32m
Richarlison	1-1	37m
MAHREZ	1-2	63m
SILVA	1-3	77m

LEICESTER CITY 0-2 MANCHESTER CITY
Saturday 3 April 2021

Victory at third placed Leicester was well deserved but City had to be patient before Benjamin Mendy opened the scoring. Kevin de Bruyne hit the bar with a free-kick, Fernandinho had a goal disallowed and Foxes keeper Kaspar Schmeichel thwarted his old teammate Riyad Mahrez. Gabriel Jesus doubled the lead as City stretched the gap at the top of the table to a gigantic 17 points.

GOALCHART

MENDY	0-1	58m
JESUS	0-2	74m

27

MANCHESTER UNITED

POSITION: RUNNERS UP

TOP SCORER: Bruno Fernandes (18)
PLAYER OF THE YEAR: Luke Shaw

BEST WINS:

MANCHESTER UNITED **9-0** SOUTHAMPTON

WORST DEFEATS:

MANCHESTER UNITED **1-6** TOTTENHAM HOTSPUR

WHAT THEY NEED:

- To maintain their superb away form. Last season United succeeded in staying unbeaten away from home in the Premier League, winning 12 of their 19 trips.

- In contrast, United must do better at home, where they only won three more games than the six they lost.

- To try and strengthen the squad so that quality remains high when top players are rotated.

QUIZ QUESTION:

Who was the Uruguay striker signed by United after he left PSG?

ANSWER

(Answer on page 61)

LIVERPOOL

POSITION:

3rd

TOP SCORER:
Mo Salah (22)

PLAYER OF THE YEAR:
Mo Salah

BEST WINS:

CRYSTAL PALACE **0-7** LIVERPOOL

WORST DEFEATS:

ASTON VILLA **7-2** LIVERPOOL

WHAT THEY NEED:

- To have Virgil van Dijk fully fit and on form again. The Reds missed their defensive kingpin last season.

- To make Anfield a fortress again. After going 68 home games without defeat, Liverpool lost six times at their own ground last term.

- To keep captain Jordan Henderson fit. Liverpool are much harder to beat when the England midfielder is there to drive them on.

QUIZ QUESTION:

Who left the club on a free transfer after playing in every Premier League game in 2020/21?

ANSWER

(Answer on page 61)

CHELSEA

POSITION:
4th

TOP SCORER:
Jorginho (7)

PLAYER OF THE YEAR:
Mason Mount

BEST WINS:
CHELSEA 4-0 CRYSTAL PALACE

WORST DEFEATS:
CHELSEA 2-5 WEST BROMWICH ALBION

WHAT THEY NEED:

- To produce a prolific scorer. Incredibly, Chelsea finished in the top four last season with top-scorer Jorginho scoring just seven goals – and even more amazingly they were all penalties!

- To get more goals from Kai Havertz and Timo Werner in particular, who cost a reported £72m and £47.7m in the summer of 2020, but contributed just 10 Premier League goals between them.

- To try to win the Premier League, or at least get closer to it. Last season Chelsea finished a gigantic 19 points off the top, despite being good enough to beat title winners Manchester City in the Champions League final as well as the semi-final of the FA Cup.

QUIZ QUESTION:

When Jorginho scored seven penalties in 2020/21 he equalled the record of which member of Liverpool's 2020/21 squad?

ANSWER

(Answer on page 61)

LEICESTER CITY

POSITION:
5th

TOP SCORER:
Jamie Vardy (15)

PLAYER OF THE YEAR:
Youri Tielemans

BEST WINS:

LEICESTER CITY **5-0** SHEFFIELD UNITED

WORST DEFEATS:

LEICESTER CITY **0-3** WEST HAM UNITED
LIVERPOOL **3-0** LEICESTER CITY

WHAT THEY NEED:

- The FA Cup winners have to deal with the disappointment of just missing out on a Champions League place and make sure they qualify this time.

- To tighten up in defence. Of the top 11, only Leeds let in as many as the 50 goals leaked by Leicester.

- To be harder to beat at home. Only the relegated clubs lost more home games in 2020/21.

QUIZ QUESTION:

In all competitions who scored even more goals for Leicester in 2020/21 than Jamie Vardy?

ANSWER

(Answer on page 61)

31

WEST HAM UNITED

POSITION:

6th

TOP SCORER:
Michail Antonio &
Tomáš Souček (10)

PLAYER OF THE YEAR:
Tomáš Souček

BEST WINS:

WEST HAM UNITED **4-0**
WOLVERHAMPTON WANDERERS

WORST DEFEATS:

CHELSEA **3-0** WEST HAM UNITED

WHAT THEY NEED:

- To maintain the improvement they showed last season when they achieved a club record Premier points haul.

- To tighten up defensively away from home. West Ham conceded as many goals as relegated Fulham.

- To acquire an outstanding goal-scorer. The Hammers did well to finish sixth with their joint-top scorers only just reaching double-figures. They need a star striker as no one has scored more than 12 Premier League goals in a season for West Ham since Marlon Harewood got 16 in 2005/06.

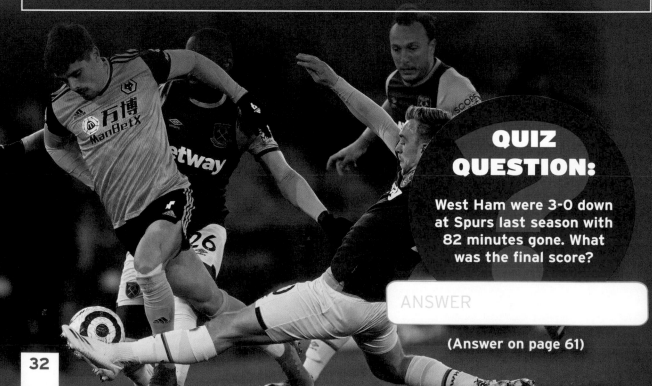

QUIZ QUESTION:

West Ham were 3-0 down at Spurs last season with 82 minutes gone. What was the final score?

ANSWER

(Answer on page 61)

TOTTENHAM HOTSPUR

POSITION:
7th

TOP SCORER:
Harry Kane (23)

PLAYER OF THE YEAR:
Harry Kane

BEST WINS:

MANCHESTER UNITED **1-6** SPURS

WORST DEFEATS:

MANCHESTER CITY **3-0** SPURS

WHAT THEY NEED:

- To settle quickly under their new manager.
- To go the distance. Last season Spurs topped the table in December after an excellent first half of the season but then fell away badly.
- To maintain their goal-scoring flair. In 2020/21 Tottenham totalled 121 goals in all competitions, 66 of them in the Premier League.

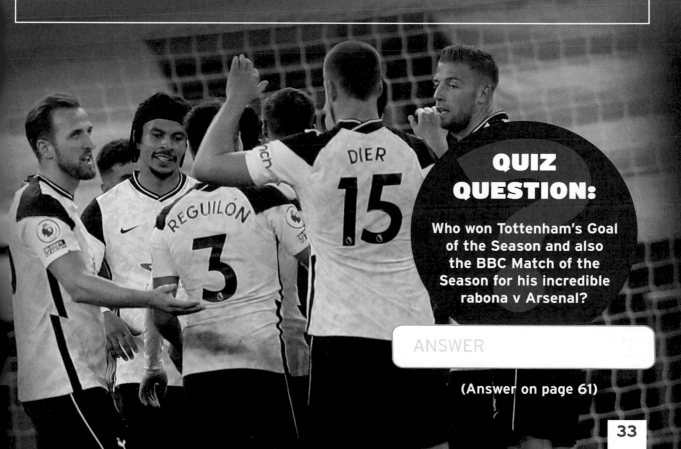

QUIZ QUESTION:

Who won Tottenham's Goal of the Season and also the BBC Match of the Season for his incredible rabona v Arsenal?

ANSWER

(Answer on page 61)

ARSENAL

POSITION:

8th

TOP SCORER:
Alexandre Lacazette (13)

PLAYER OF THE YEAR:
Bukayo Saka

BEST WINS:

WEST BROMWICH ALBION **0-4** ARSENAL

WORST DEFEATS:

ARSENAL **0-3** ASTON VILLA
ARSENAL **0-3** LIVERPOOL

WHAT THEY NEED:

- To qualify for Europe after failing to do so for the first time since 1994/95.

- To improve at home. Ten games were won away with only six defeats, but at home there were only eight victories but seven losses.

- Continue to allow their young talent, such as Bukayo Saka and Emile Smith Rowe, to blossom.

QUIZ QUESTION:

Which Brazil international and former Premier League winner with Chelsea left the Gunners in the summer?

ANSWER

(Answer on page 61)

LEEDS UNITED

POSITION:
9th

TOP SCORER:
Patrick Bamford (17)

PLAYER OF THE YEAR:
Stuart Dallas

BEST WINS:

WEST BROMWICH ALBION **0-5** LEEDS UNITED

WORST DEFEATS:

MANCHESTER UNITED **6-2** LEEDS UNITED

WHAT THEY NEED:

- To avoid second season syndrome. Leeds did very well in their first season after promotion - but Sheffield United also finished ninth in 2019/20 after promotion, and then finished bottom.

- To make sure they retain head coach Marcelo Bielsa who has been credited with so much of Leeds' organisation, quality and flair.

- Having had more goals in their Premier League games last season than exciting champions Manchester City, Leeds need to maintain their reputation for entertaining football.

QUIZ QUESTION:

Which Leeds player won his first seven England caps during the 2020/21 season?

ANSWER

(Answer on page 61)

EVERTON

POSITION:

10th

TOP SCORER:
Dominic Calvert-Lewin (16)

PLAYER OF THE YEAR:
Dominic Calvert-Lewin

BEST WINS:

EVERTON **5-2** WEST BROMWICH ALBION

WORST DEFEATS:

MANCHESTER CITY **5-0** EVERTON

WHAT THEY NEED:

- To bounce back from the shock of the sudden departure of high-profile manager Carlo Ancelotti.

- To keep faith with Jordan Pickford – England's best goalkeeper.

- To keep supplying centre-forward Dominic Calvert-Lewin who led the line so well last season.

QUIZ QUESTION:

Who scored a third minute goal as Everton beat Liverpool 2-0 at Anfield in February 2021?

ANSWER

(Answer on page 61)

ASTON VILLA

POSITION:
11th

TOP SCORER:
Ollie Watkins (14)

PLAYER OF THE YEAR:
Emiliano Martínez

BEST WINS:

ASTON VILLA 7-2 LIVERPOOL

WORST DEFEATS:

ASTON VILLA 0-3 LEEDS UNITED

WHAT THEY NEED:

- To improve on their good season last term when they climbed to 11th after the previous finish of 17th after winning promotion.

- Improve their home form. Villa conceded eight more goals at home than they did away last season and won five fewer points at Villa Park than they did on the road.

- Carefully nurture the stars of tomorrow who won the FA Youth Cup.

QUIZ QUESTION:

Which London club did Villa sign player of the year Emiliano Martinez from?

ANSWER

(Answer on page 61)

NEWCASTLE UNITED

POSITION:
12th

TOP SCORER:
Callum Wilson (12)

PLAYER OF THE YEAR:
Callum Wilson

BEST WINS:

LEICESTER **2-4** NEWCASTLE
NEWCASTLE **3-1** BURNLEY
WEST HAM **0-2** NEWCASTLE
CRYSTAL PALACE **0-2** NEWCASTLE
EVERTON **0-2** NEWCASTLE
FULHAM **0-2** NEWCASTLE

WORST DEFEATS:

LEEDS **5-2** NEWCASTLE
NEWCASTLE **1-4** MANCHESTER UNITED
ARSENAL **3-0** NEWCASTLE
NEWCASTLE **0-3** BRIGHTON
BRIGHTON **3-0** NEWCASTLE

WHAT THEY NEED:

- To improve their defence, especially at home. Only relegated West Brom conceded more goals on their own patch than the Magpies last season.

- To get Allan Saint-Maximin to produce more – he only scored three goals last season.

- To have more goals around the team. Other than the on-loan Gunner, Joe Willock, only Callum scored more than four goals.

QUIZ QUESTION:

Which player on loan from Arsenal scored in all of the last seven games to equal Alan Shearer's club record?

ANSWER

(Answer on page 61)

WOLVERHAMPTON WANDERERS

POSITION:
13th

TOP SCORER:
Pedro Neto &
Rúben Neves (5)

PLAYER OF THE YEAR:
Pedro Neto

BEST WINS:

SHEFFIELD UTD **0-2** WOLVES
WOLVES **2-0** CRYSTAL PALACE

WORST DEFEATS:

WEST HAM **4-0** WOLVES
LIVERPOOL **4-0** WOLVES
WOLVES **0-4** BURNLEY

WHAT THEY NEED:

- More goals: only twice did they win by two goals last season, including the first game of the season at doomed Sheffield Utd. Only the bottom four scored fewer goals overall.

- To be able to score away from home. Only bottom of the table Sheffield United scored fewer than Wolves' 15 away goals.

- A striker. After Raúl Jiménez's serious injury, no-one managed more than five goals.

QUIZ QUESTION:

Rui Patrício and which other player missed just one Premier League game?

ANSWER

(Answer on page 61)

CRYSTAL PALACE

POSITION:

14th

TOP SCORER:
Wilfried Zaha (11)

PLAYER OF THE YEAR:
Vicente Guaita

BEST WINS:

WBA **1-5** CRYSTAL PALACE

WORST DEFEATS:

CRYSTAL PALACE **0-7** LIVERPOOL

WHAT THEY NEED:

- To establish a new identity under new management after the retirement of Roy Hodgson.

- To develop the talent of Eberechi Eze who had such a good season in the Premier League after moving from QPR.

- To improve at both ends – last season only the bottom three had a poorer goal difference than Palace's -25.

QUIZ QUESTION:

Which player other than top scorer Wilfried Zaha also got into double figures for Premier League goals for Palace in 2020/21?

ANSWER

(Answer on page 61)

SOUTHAMPTON

POSITION:

15th

TOP SCORER:
Danny Ings (12)

PLAYER OF THE YEAR:
James Ward-Prowse

BEST WINS:

SOUTHAMPTON **3-0** SHEFFIELD UTD

WORST DEFEATS:

MANCHESTER UNITED **9-0** SOUTHAMPTON

WHAT THEY NEED:

- To go a whole season without conceding nine goals in a single game as they have done in the last two seasons.

- Become more difficult to beat away from home. Last season, only the bottom two lost as many games on the road than the Saints. Even relegated Fulham lost four fewer away games.

- To revel in regaining their identity with a return to their traditional red and white stripes in their 2021/22 Hummel kit.

QUIZ QUESTION:

Which Champions League team did Southampton beat in their first game of the calendar year of 2021?

ANSWER

(Answer on page 61)

41

BRIGHTON & HOVE ALBION

POSITION:

16th

TOP SCORER:
Neal Maupay (8)

PLAYER OF THE YEAR:
Lewis Dunk

BEST WINS:

NEWCASTLE UNITED **0-3** BRIGHTON & HOVE ALBION
BRIGHTON & HOVE ALBION **3-0** NEWCASTLE UNITED

WORST DEFEATS:

LEICESTER CITY **3-0** BRIGHTON & HOVE ALBION

WHAT THEY NEED:

- To win more than nine games. The Seagulls have stuck on nine victories in each of their four seasons since promotion.

- To improve their home form. Brighton won just four home games at the Amex in 2020/21.

- To maintain improvement at both ends. Last season, Albion created club records of scoring 40 Premier League goals and conceding only 46 – only six sides had a better defence. Now they need to tip the balance to a positive goal difference.

QUIZ QUESTION:

Who were Albion playing when they set a Premier League record of hitting the woodwork five times and then lost 2-3 when VAR awarded a penalty against Neal Maupay after what was meant to be the final whistle?

ANSWER

(Answer on page 61)

BURNLEY

POSITION:

17th

TOP SCORER:
Chris Wood (12)

PLAYER OF THE YEAR:
Chris Wood

BEST WINS:

WOLVES **0-4** BURNLEY

WORST DEFEATS:

MANCHESTER CITY **5-0** BURNLEY

WHAT THEY NEED:

- To get off to a better start. Last season only one point was taken from the first six games – and that from West Bromwich Albion who went on to be relegated.

- Score more goals. Despite Chris Wood's 12, the Clarets only scored 33 in total - fewer than West Brom who went down and the worst of the 17 teams who retained their Premier League status.

- Improve home form. Without the backing of their fans due to COVID-19, Burnley picked up under a point a game at Turf Moor.

QUIZ QUESTION:

Who was the Burnley goalkeeper who missed out on England's European Championships squad because of injury?

ANSWER

(Answer on page 61)

MANCHESTER

The two biggest transfers of the summer transfer window brought superstars Cristiano Ronaldo and Jack Grealish to Manchester - Ronaldo back to Old Trafford and Grealish to City. While Chelsea also re-signed Romelu Lukaku from Inter Milan for £97.5m, Grealish had just become The Premier League's first £100m player. Like Lukaku, Ronaldo arrived from Italian football but, while his move from Juventus did not involve such a big fee given his age, there is no doubt he is one of the greatest footballers of all time. City and United were already the top two teams in the Premier League but, with Grealish and Ronaldo added to their ranks, the Manchester Marvels will be even better.

GREALISH

With his child size shinpads, his socks half-way down his tanned and muscular calves and his hair flowing over his hairband Jack Grealish is unmissable. With the ball at his feet you know he is either going to create a goal, score one himself or be fouled for a dangerous free-kick. Last season, when he was at Aston Villa, Grealish was fouled more times than any other player - 22 times more than the Premier League's second most fouled footballer Wilfred Zaha. With City's array of dead-ball experts fouls on him will result in even more set-piece goals.

Capped 12 times with England before coming to City.

Played in the delayed Euro 2020 final for England against Italy.

Capped up to Under 21 level by the Republic of Ireland before deciding to play for England, the country of his birth.

Republic of Ireland's Under 17 international Player of the Year in 2012 and Under 21 Player of the Year award winner in 2015.

Jack's great-great grandfather Billy Garraty played for England and won the FA Cup with Aston Villa in 1905.

Jack made his senior debut for Notts County at MK Dons on 14 September 2013 while on loan from Villa.

Started 157 games for Villa, appeared 49 times as a substitute and scored 32 goals.

Aston Villa's Player of the Season in 2019-20

Made his debut for City at Wembley in the Community Shield against Leicester City.

Scored his first goal for the club on his home debut in a 5-0 victory over Norwich City.

44

MARVELS

RONALDO

Originally with Manchester United from 2003 to 2009, Ronaldo then spent a decade with Real Madrid and three years with Juventus having begun his career with Sporting Lisbon. For more than a decade he has vied with Lionel Messi for the accolade of being the world's best player. Ole Gunner Solskjær is in no doubt. The United boss declared, "He's the greatest player of all time if you ask me." Ronaldo will be 37 on 5 February but, because he has always looked after himself, still looks in peak condition. A brilliant goal-scorer, Ronaldo scores all kinds of goals and unlike so many hugely skilful players is also excellent in the air. He was a young player when he was at Old Trafford before and now has so much more experience. Will he be better than before as a Red Devil? Time will tell but like Grealish he will be a Manchester Marvel.

Ballon d'Or (Best Player in the World) Winner: 2008, 2013, 2014, 2016 & 2017

FIFA World Player of the Year: 2008

European Golden Shoe (Top Scorer) Winner: 2007-08, 2010-11, 2013-14 & 2014-15

Premier League Golden Boot Winner: 2007-08

Serie A Footballer of the Year: 2019 & 2020

Capocannoniere (Serie A Top-Scorer) Winner: 2020-21

Euro 2016 Winner with Portugal

Three Premier League titles, Champions League and FIFA World Club Cup, FA Cup and two League Cups with Manchester United.

Four Champions League titles, Three FIFA World Club Cups, two UEFA Super Cups, two La Liga titles, two Copa del Reys and two Spanish Supercups with Real Madrid.

Two Serie A titles, two Italian Supercups and the Coppa Italia with Juventus.

SPOT THE DIFFERENCE

Can you spot the ten differences in these photos from when Burnley took on Liverpool in February 2021?

PREMIER POSERS

How well do you know the Premier League? Test yourself on these questions - but be warned, the questions get harder as you go.

1 Which club has won the Premier League the most times?

2 Who is the only club to have won the Premier League who is not currently in it?

3 Which London clubs have won the Premier League?

4 How many different clubs have won the Premier League?

5 How many of the clubs who have won the Premier League can you name?

6 Who became the 50th club to play in the Premier League when they played in the opening Premier League game of this season against Arsenal?

7 The clubs who have been relegated from the Premier League the most times swapped places in 2021. One went down and the other came up. Name the clubs.

8 How many of the clubs who have ever won the Premier League have ever been relegated from it?

9 Can you name them?

10 Can you name the three teams who were relegated in the same season that they topped the Premier League?

11 Known as 'The Invincibles', who is the only club to go a whole Premier League season without defeat?

12 Which club once won 100 points in a Premier League season?

13 What strange feat did Bobby Zamora and Obafemi Martins achieve with Premier League penalties?

14 Who set a record by missing 11 Premier League penalties?

15 What do George Boyd, David Nugent, Steve Kabba and Mark Robins all have in common?

16 What links Hull City (2009/10), Derby County (2007/08), Norwich City (2004/05), Wolves (2003/04), Coventry City (1999/00) and Leeds United (1992/93)?

17 Which two clubs have played in every Premier League season but have never won it?

18 How many times have none of the teams promoted to the Premier League been relegated in their first season?

19 In 2020/21 Sheffield United only scored 20 goals. Who are the only club to score as few goals in a Premier League season?

20 Only one club has conceded 100 goals in a Premier League season. Who did this in 1993/94?

Answers on page 61.

PREVIOUS

The Premier League attracts some of the biggest stars from all over the globe. While Kevin De Bruyne, Sadio Mané, Harry Kane, and Jamie Vardy are amongst the biggest names now, do you remember these previous Premier League superstars?

THIERRY HENRY

- Arsenal 1999-2007
- 254 Games
- 174 Goals
- 8 Premier League Hat-Tricks
- 228 Arsenal Goals in Total
- Gunners' All-Time Record Scorer.
- Two Premier League Titles
- FIFA World Cup Winner with France 1998
- Pace and Prolific Scoring

ERIC CANTONA

- Manchester United 1992-1997
- 143 Man Utd Games
- 64 Man Utd Goals
- 4 Premier League Titles with Man Utd
- Style and Skill

PREMIER

ROY KEANE

- Manchester United 1993-2005
- 326 Games
- 33 Goals
- 7 Premier League Titles
- Power, Control and Midfield Dominance

DIDIER DROGBA

- Chelsea 2004-2012 & 2014-15
- 254 Games
- 104 Goals
- 4 Premier League Titles
- Strength and Skill

JUNINHO

- Middlesbrough 1995-1997, 1999-2000 & 2002-2004
- 120 Games
- 27 Goals
- Helped Middlesbrough to their Only Ever Trophy (2004 League Cup)
- Brazilian Flair with Toughness and a Smile!

SPOT THE SEASON

Put your Premier League knowledge to the test!
Can you work out the season based on the facts?

LEICESTER CITY stunned football by winning their first ever top-flight title.

ARSENAL, SPURS AND MANCHESTER CITY joined **LEICESTER** in qualifying for the Champions League.

LEICESTER landed a double of Premier League Manager of the Season and Player of the Season with Claudio Ranieri and James Vardy winning the awards.

HARRY KANE was the Premier League's top scorer with 25 goals – one ahead of Sergio Agüero and Jamie Vardy.

Mesut Özil's 19 assists made him the top assist maker with six more than anyone else. Only Cesc Fàbregas and Andrew Surman made more passes than Özil's 2,205.

N'GOLO KANTÉ, then of Leicester made the most tackles (175) and interceptions (157) in the Premier League.

Manchester United beat Newcastle United 6-1 at Old Trafford in the season's

BIGGEST HOME WIN.

ARSENAL'S Petr Čech kept the most clean sheets. His 16 was one more than David de Gea of Man Utd, Joe Hart of Man City and Kasper Schmeichel of the champions Leicester.

ASTON VILLA lost 6-0 at Villa Park against **LIVERPOOL** in the season's biggest home defeat.

LIVERPOOL also scored five at Carrow Road in beating **NORWICH CITY** 5-4 in the highest scoring game of the season.

WEST HAM played their last season at the Boleyn Ground.

NEWCASTLE UNITED, NORWICH CITY and **ASTON VILLA** were relegated.

SUNDERLAND spent more days (237) in the bottom three than any club but stayed up, their win over **EVERTON** confirming the relegation of **NORWICH** and local rivals **NEWCASTLE**.

José Mourinho was sacked by defending champions Chelsea and **Brendan Rodgers** was dismissed by Liverpool.

Your Answer:

(Answer on page 61)

ASSIST KINGS

Playmakers, schemers, fantasistas, creators. Call them what you will - it is the players who can conjure up goal-scoring chances that make teams tick. It is not much use having a superb striker if no-one can get the ball to him, or if the service to the forward does not bring the best out of him. If a striker wants the ball played to his feet, there's not much point hitting high balls, and if a front-man is brilliant in the air, he needs balls he can attack. It is having the talent and vision to produce penetrating telling passes that makes people assist kings.

HARRY KANE

So, who sets up the most goals in the Premier League? In 2020/21 these were the top 12 with the number of goals they provided assists for.

PLAYER	GOALS ASSISTED
Harry Kane	14
Bruno Fernandes	12
Kevin De Bruyne	12
Jack Grealish	10
Son Heung-min	10
Raphinha	9
Marcus Rashford	9
Jamie Vardy	9
Aaron Cresswell	8
Pascal Groß	8
Jack Harrison	8
Timo Werner	8

HARRY KANE

was out in front as the best in the league - just as he was in the scoring charts as he won the Golden Boot. Kane contributed 14 assists, two more than the Manchester pair of United's Bruno Fernandes and City's Kevin De Bruyne. Only two other players reached double figures: Jack Grealish of Aston Villa (now Man City) and Kane's Tottenham teammate Son Heung-min.

KEVIN DE BRUYNE

JACK GREALISH

BRUNO FERNANDES

MARCUS RASHFORD

Pascal Groß

Leeds United thrilled many football fans with their stylish play with the Whites' brilliant Brazilian **Raphinha** assisting nine goals, one more than his Elland Road teammate Jack Harrison.

Marcus Rashford has been doing a lot of great work to help others off the pitch and the England forward has made a habit of helping others on the pitch as well. The Manchester United and England man set up nine goals, as did Leicester City striker **Jamie Vardy** who remains more than a handful for any defence.

West Ham's good season saw **Aaron Cresswell** create eight goals while Chelsea's expensive **Timo Werner** made the same number. Playing in a successful team helps players in the assists table. Schemers in top sides see their passes met by top strikers who can make the most of them. **Jack Grealish** did well to set up 10 goals for Aston Villa who finished 11th, while all the other members of the assists top 12 played for clubs who finished in the top half of the table – except for one man.

Well done to **Pascal Groß** of Brighton and Hove Albion. Not only did the Seagulls finish just two places above the drop zone, but as a team they scored just 40 goals   the same number that Harry Kane and Son Heung-Min scored for Spurs. German midfielder Groß set up eight goals for low-scoring Brighton. It wasn't the first time he has stood out in a struggling team. In 2016/17 playing for Ingolstadt in the Bundesliga, Groß created more chances than anyone in the league even though his team were relegated. That summer he cost Brighton £3m, a rare bargain in modern football especially as assist kings are worth their weight in 'goal-d.'

FIRST
ELEVEN

The Premier League doesn't just attract the best players in the world, it also brings the best managers to English football.

DID YOU KNOW?
An English manager has never won the Premier League!

There have been 29 Premier League seasons before this one, but only 11 managers have ever led their team to the trophy. Pep Guardiola and Jürgen Klopp have managed the last two title winning teams and their sides have done it in style. With top class managers such as Thomas Tuchel, Brendan Rodgers and Marcelo Bielsa looking to join the list of 11 Premier League winning bosses, the challenge to be the man who takes his team to the title is as fierce as ever.

Eighty years old as of New Year's Eve going into 2022, Sir Alex Ferguson has won 10 more Premier League titles than anyone else. 'Fergie' won the Premier League 13 times with Manchester United. Last season, Pep Guardiola won his third title with Manchester City joining José Mourinho, who won three with Chelsea, and Arsène Wenger who won three with Arsenal. No other manager has succeeded in winning more than a single Premier League title.

Only two men have managed in more than 650 Premier League fixtures: Sir Alex Ferguson, who was in charge of 810 games for Manchester United, but even he can't quite equal the 828 matches Arsène Wenger had at Arsenal.

Although no English manager has ever won the Premier League, almost half the people who had ever managed in the Premier League up to the end of last season were English. 121 English managers have tried to win the crown without success, while 126 other managers from around the world have also brought their talent and tactics to the world's most glamourous league.

PREMIER LEAGUE TITLES
BY MANAGER NATIONALITY

SCOTLAND	14	Sir Alex Ferguson (13) Kenny Dalglish (1)
ITALY	4	Carlo Ancelotti, Antonio Conte, Roberto Mancini & Claudio Ranieri
FRANCE	3	Arsène Wenger (3)
PORTUGAL	3	José Mourinho (3)
SPAIN	3	Pep Guardiola (3)
CHILE	1	Manuel Pellegrini
GERMANY	1	Jürgen Klopp

PREMIER LEAGUE MANAGERS
BY COUNTRY
(To the end of 2020/21)

Country	Managers
ENGLAND	121
SCOTLAND	36
ITALY	12
SPAIN	10
WALES	9
NETHERLANDS	8
NORTHERN IRELAND	7
FRANCE	6
REPUBLIC OF IRELAND	6
GERMANY	5
PORTUGAL	5
ARGENTINA	4
SWEDEN	3
CROATIA	2
NORWAY	2
USA	2
AUSTRIA	1
BRAZIL	1
CHILE	1
DENMARK	1
ISRAEL	1
JAMAICA	1
SERBIA	1
SWITZERLAND	1
URUGUAY	1

SEVENTH HELL &

Liverpool's title defence saw the Reds struggle to stay in the race to retain the Premier League crown. There were seven goals in the Reds opening Premier League game as they beat Leeds 4-3 and, 12 days later, seven were scored as Lincoln were lashed 7-2 in the Carabao Cup, only for Jürgen Klopp's men to amazingly concede seven in their next away game at Villa. Just before Christmas, Liverpool played like champions in winning 7-0 away to Palace as Liverpool went from seventh hell to seventh heaven.

ASTON VILLA 7-2 LIVERPOOL

Villa Park ———————————— 4 October 2020

Ollie Watkins bagged a first half hat-trick.

Jack Grealish scored the last two goals and had a hand in three others.

Villa hadn't beaten the reigning champions since beating Arsenal in December 1998.

Liverpool let in seven goals for the first time since 1963 when they lost 7-2 to Spurs.

Watkins went into the game without a Premier League goal to his name.

Watkins' hat-trick was the first Premier League hat-trick scored against Liverpool since Dimitar Berbatov did so for Manchester United 10 years earlier.

Liverpool became the first champions to concede seven goals in a match since Arsenal lost 7-1 at Sunderland in 1953.

Mo Salah's brace were a mere consolation for the champions.

Former Everton man Ross Barkley scored against Liverpool with a 20-yarder on his Villa debut.

Villa went second after three games – it was their best start since 1962.

GOALCHART

Villa 1-0 Liverpool	Ollie Watkins	4m
Villa 2-0 Liverpool	Ollie Watkins	22m
Villa 2-1 Liverpool	Mo Salah	33m
Villa 3-1 Liverpool	John McGinn	35m
Villa 4-1 Liverpool	Ollie Watkins	39m
Villa 5-1 Liverpool	Ross Barkley	55m
Villa 5-2 Liverpool	Mo Salah	60m
Villa 6-2 Liverpool	Jack Grealish	66m
Villa 7-2 Liverpool	Jack Grealish	75m

SEVENTH HEAVEN

CRYSTAL PALACE 0-7 LIVERPOOL

Selhurst Park ——————— 19 December 2020

It was the first time Liverpool had ever won a top flight away game by seven goals.

It was the first time Palace had ever conceded seven times in a home game.

At the time Liverpool were eight points clear of Manchester City, who had one game in hand.

Back in the groove, the champions went five points clear at the top of the table.

In achieving his 127th win as Liverpool boss, Jürgen Klopp overtook Rafa Benítez's total as Reds boss.

The Reds scored seven in a top flight away game for the first time since a 1991 trip to Derby.

Japan international Takumi Minamino scored his first Premier League goal.

For the first time in Premier League history, seven different players claimed assists in the same game for one team: Mané, Firmino, Robertson, Alexander-Arnold, Salah, Matip and Oxlade-Chamberlain.

GOALCHART

Palace 0-1 Liverpool	Takumi Minamino	3m
Palace 0-2 Liverpool	Sadio Mané	35m
Palace 0-3 Liverpool	Roberto Firmino	44m
Palace 0-4 Liverpool	Jordan Henderson	52m
Palace 0-5 Liverpool	Roberto Firmino	68m
Palace 0-6 Liverpool	Mo Salah	81m
Palace 0-7 Liverpool	Mo Salah	84m

25 October 2019

SOUTHAMPTON 0-9 LEICESTER CITY

GOAL COUNT

10m	Ben Chilwell
17m	Youri Tielemans
19m	Ayoze Perez
39m	Ayoze Perez
45m	Jamie Vardy
57m	Ayoze Perez
58m	Jamie Vardy
85m	James Maddison
90+4	Jamie Vardy *(pen)*

RED CARD

Southampton were reduced to 10 men in the 12th minute when Ryan Bertrand was sent off.

Leicester had 25 shots and 73% possession.

Saints players and coaching staff gave their wages from the day of the game to the Saints Foundation.

In the reverse fixture three months later at Leicester, Southampton won 2-1!

STAT FACT

The Foxes set a new record for the biggest ever away win in the English top flight. This was previously held by Sunderland's 9-1 win at Newcastle in 1908 and Wolves' 9-1 win at Cardiff in 1955.

STAT FACT

Ayoze Perez and Jamie Vardy both scored hat-tricks. It was only the second time that two players had scored hat-tricks for the same team in a Premier League game. The other occasion was in May 2003 when Arsenal's Jermaine Pennant and Robert Pires scored in a 6-1 win over... Southampton!

SINNERS

MANCHESTER UNITED 9-0 SOUTHAMPTON

GOAL COUNT

18m	Aaron Wan-Bissaka
25m	Marcus Rashford
34m	Jan Bednarek *own goal*
39m	Edinson Cavani
69m	Anthony Martial
71m	Scott McTominay
87m	Bruno Fernandes *(pen)*
90m	Anthony Martial
90+1	Daniel James

RED CARDS

Southampton were reduced to 10 men in only the 2nd minute when Alex Jankewitz was sent off. They ended the game with nine men when Jan Bednarek was dismissed four minutes from time, when it was 6-0.

Manchester United had 24 shots and 75% possession.

United equalled their record Premier League victory of 9-0 against Ipswich Town in March 1995.

In the reverse fixture just over months earlier at Southampton, Saints led 2-0 at half-time – and lost 2-3.

STAT FACT

This was the biggest away defeat in Southampton's history. Previously they had lost 8-0 at Everton in 1971 and at Tottenham Hotspur in 1936.

STAT FACT

United had seven scorers, equalling Chelsea's record set against Aston Villa in 2012.

PREMIER LEAGUE
Fun Facts

Nine of the teams in the Premier League in 2020/21 spent some of the season at the top of the table. It was the first time so many sides had been table-toppers in a Premier League campaign.

There were 33 1-0 home wins and 38 1-0 away wins.

The 1000th own goal in the history of the Premier League was scored by Tottenham's Sergio Reguilón in a game against Aston Villa in May 2021.

There were more goals scored by home teams than away games: 514 to 510.

There were 60 more second half goals than first half goals: 542 to 482.

Harry Kane and Raheem Sterling were both born in the year the Premier League began in 1992.

Leeds pipped Everton and Newcastle pipped Wolves on goal difference in the 2020/21 Premier League table.

Saints or sinners...?

Southampton's 9-0 loss at Manchester United saw seven different Red Devils get on the score-sheet.

Leeds became the 30th different Premier League team Harry Kane had scored against when he netted against them in 2021. No other player has scored against as many other clubs in the Premier League.

Kelechi Iheanacho scored a goal on every day of the week in 2020/21. He became the first player to achieve that in a single season.

270 players scored in the Premier League in 2020/21.

Champions beware of the Saints. Arsenal, Blackburn Rovers, Chelsea, Leicester City, Liverpool, Manchester City and Manchester United are the seven teams to have won the Premier League. Southampton have beaten them all in the season after they have won their first titles.

With most games played behind closed doors and no crowds to urge on home sides, there were more away wins than home wins in the Premier League in 2020/21. There were 37.89% home wins and 40.26% away wins.

Mr. Consistency.

Dead ball specialist James Ward-Prowse played every minute of the Premier League campaign in 2020/21 – for the second successive season! No-one had ever done that before.

Manchester leads Merseyside by 18 to 1 in terms of Premier League titles. United have been champions 13 times and City five times. Liverpool have been champions once with Everton yet to win the trophy.

QUIZ & PUZZLE ANSWERS

PAGE 18-19:
Spot the Season: 2011/12

PAGE 24-25
Manchester City:
Raheem Sterling

PAGE 28
Manchester United:
Edinson Cavani

PAGE 29
Liverpool:
Georginio Wijnaldum

PAGE 30
Chelsea: James Milner

PAGE 31
Leicester City:
Kelechi Iheanacho

PAGE 32
West Ham: 3-3

PAGE 33
Spurs: Érik Lamela

PAGE 34
Arsenal: David Luiz

PAGE 35
Leeds Utd: Kalvin Phillips

PAGE 36
Everton: Richarlison

PAGE 37
Aston Villa: Arsenal

PAGE 38
Newcastle Utd: Joe Willock

PAGE 39
Wolves: Conor Coady

PAGE 40
Crystal Palace:
Christian Benteke

PAGE 41
Southampton: Liverpool

PAGE 42
Brighton & Hove Albion:
Manchester United

PAGE 43
Burnley: Nick Pope

PAGE 46: SPOT THE DIFFERENCE

PAGE 47:
Premier League Posers

1 Manchester United (13)
2 Blackburn Rovers
3 Arsenal and Chelsea
4 Seven
5 Arsenal, Blackburn Rovers, Chelsea, Leicester City, Liverpool, Manchester City & Manchester United.
6 Brentford
7 West Bromwich Albion and Norwich City
8 Three
9 Blackburn Rovers, Leicester City and Manchester City.
10 Hull City (2016/17), Bolton Wanderers (2011/12) and Charlton Athletic (1998/99).
11 Arsenal (In 2003/04)
12 Manchester City (2017/2018)
13 They scored them with right foot and left foot shots.
14 Alan Shearer
15 They have all played for two clubs that were relegated from the Premier League in the same season.
16 None of them won an away game in a Premier League campaign.
17 Everton and Tottenham Hotspur
18 Three 2001/02, 2011/12 and 2017/18
19 Derby County 2007/08
20 Swindon Town

PAGE 50-51: Spot the Season
2015/16 season